The Adaptive Industrialist: Mastering Change in a Dynamic World

Jones

Copyright © [2023]

Title: The Adaptive Industrialist: Mastering Change in a Dynamic World
Author's: Jones

All rights reserved. No part of this publication may be reproduced, stored in a retrieval system, or transmitted in any form or by any means, electronic, mechanical, photocopying, recording, or otherwise, without the prior written permission of the publisher or author, except in the case of brief quotations embodied in critical reviews and certain other non-commercial uses permitted by copyright law.

This book was printed and published by [Publisher's: **Jones**] in [2023]

ISBN:

TABLE OF CONTENT

Chapter 1: Understanding the Industrial Landscape   07

The Evolution of the Industrial Landscape

The Impact of Technology on Industries

The Current State of the Industrial Landscape

Chapter 2: The Need for Adaptation and Change   13

Recognizing the Need for Adaptation

Embracing Disruption in the Industrial Landscape

The Dangers of Resisting Change

Chapter 3: Developing an Adaptive Mindset   19

The Importance of a Growth Mindset

Overcoming Fear and Resistance to Change

Cultivating a Curious and Open Mind

Chapter 4: Embracing Innovation in the Industrial World 25

The Role of Innovation in Adaptation

Embracing Technological Advancements

Leveraging Data and Analytics

Chapter 5: Building Resilience in the Face of Change 31

Understanding the Impact of Change on Individuals and Organizations

Developing Resilience Skills

Creating an Agile and Flexible Workforce

Chapter 6: Navigating Disruption in the Industrial Landscape 37

Understanding Disruptive Forces

Identifying Opportunities within Disruption

Strategies for Thriving in a Disrupted Industry

Chapter 7: Leading Through Change and Uncertainty 43

The Role of Leadership in Times of Change

Communicating Effectively During Transitions

Building Trust and Inspiring Others

Chapter 8: Harnessing Collaboration and Partnerships 49

The Power of Collaboration in Adaptation

Establishing Strategic Partnerships

Leveraging Networks and Alliances

Chapter 9: Overcoming Challenges in the Adaptive Journey 55

Common Challenges in Adapting to Change

Strategies for Overcoming Resistance and Obstacles

Learning from Failure and Iterating

Chapter 10: Sustaining Adaptation in a Dynamic World 61

Creating a Culture of Continuous Adaptation

The Role of Learning and Development

Nurturing Long-Term Adaptation Strategies

Chapter 11: The Future of the Adaptive Industrialist 67

Anticipating Future Trends and Disruptive Forces

The Skills and Mindset of the Future Industrialist

Paving the Way for a Sustainable and Adaptive Future

Conclusion: Mastering Change in a Dynamic World 73

Chapter 1: Understanding the Industrial Landscape

The Evolution of the Industrial Landscape

In the dynamic world we live in today, the industrial landscape is constantly evolving and adapting to new challenges and opportunities. The mind set of industrialists plays a crucial role in navigating these changes and ensuring success in a rapidly changing environment.

The industrial landscape has come a long way from its early days, where factories and manufacturing plants dominated the scene. The advent of technology and the digital revolution has transformed the way industries operate, creating new opportunities and challenges for industrialists.

One of the key drivers of change in the industrial landscape is innovation. Industrialists must constantly innovate to stay competitive and meet the ever-changing needs of customers. This may involve adopting new technologies, improving processes, or developing new products and services. The ability to embrace and drive innovation is a critical factor for success in today's industrial landscape.

Another important aspect of the evolution of the industrial landscape is sustainability. As the world becomes more conscious of the environmental impact of industrial activities, industrialists must adapt their practices to ensure sustainability. This may involve implementing eco-friendly manufacturing processes, reducing waste and emissions, or investing in renewable energy sources. By prioritizing sustainability, industrialists can not only contribute to a greener planet but also gain a competitive advantage by appealing to socially and environmentally conscious consumers.

Furthermore, globalization has had a profound impact on the industrial landscape. The interconnected nature of the global economy provides opportunities for industrialists to tap into new markets and collaborate with international partners. However, it also brings intense competition from global players. Industrialists need to develop a global mindset, understand diverse markets, and adapt their strategies accordingly to leverage the benefits of globalization.

In conclusion, the industrial landscape has evolved significantly over time, driven by factors such as innovation, sustainability, and globalization. To succeed in this ever-changing environment, industrialists must cultivate a mindset that embraces change, innovation, and sustainability. By staying ahead of the curve and adapting their strategies to fit the evolving industrial landscape, industrialists can thrive in a dynamic world and lead their industries to new heights.

The Impact of Technology on Industries

In today's fast-paced and ever-evolving world, technology has become an integral part of our lives, transforming the way we live, work, and interact. Industries across the globe have felt the profound impact of technological advancements, revolutionizing the way they operate and forcing them to adapt or risk becoming obsolete. This subchapter explores the transformative power of technology on industries and its implications for the mindset of industrialists.

The advent of technology has revolutionized the way industries function, leading to increased efficiency, productivity, and innovation. Automation, artificial intelligence, and robotics have streamlined processes, minimizing human error and allowing for faster production. This has not only reduced costs but has also resulted in higher quality products and services. Industries that have embraced technology have gained a competitive edge, enabling them to stay ahead in the market.

Furthermore, technology has opened up new avenues for industries to explore and expand. The internet, for instance, has paved the way for e-commerce, allowing businesses to reach a global audience with ease. This has led to the emergence of new industries and business models, disrupting traditional sectors. Industrialists must be open to embracing these technological advancements and adapting their strategies to capitalize on the opportunities presented.

However, with these advancements come challenges. The rapid pace of technological change requires industrialists to be agile and adaptable. The mindset of industrialists must shift from a traditional, rigid approach to a more flexible and innovative one. They must be willing to invest in research and development, constantly staying updated with the latest technological trends, and embracing change as an opportunity for growth.

Moreover, the impact of technology extends beyond operational aspects. It has also brought about significant changes in consumer behavior and expectations. Industries must understand and cater to the evolving needs and preferences of tech-savvy consumers. This requires industrialists to develop a customer-centric mindset, leveraging technology to provide personalized experiences, seamless interactions, and timely delivery of products and services.

In conclusion, the impact of technology on industries cannot be understated. It has transformed the way industries operate, opened up new opportunities, and disrupted traditional sectors. Industrialists must adopt a mindset that embraces change, innovation, and agility to thrive in this dynamic landscape. By understanding and harnessing the power of technology, industries can unlock their full potential and remain relevant in an ever-changing world.

The Current State of the Industrial Landscape

In today's dynamic world, the industrial landscape is constantly evolving and adapting to new challenges and opportunities. As the global economy becomes more interconnected, the traditional approach to industrialization is no longer sufficient. To thrive in this ever-changing environment, industrialists must embrace a new mindset and master the art of change.

One of the key aspects of the current state of the industrial landscape is the rapid pace of technological advancement. Innovations such as artificial intelligence, automation, and the Internet of Things are revolutionizing industries across the board. Industrialists must be willing to adopt and integrate these technologies into their operations to stay competitive and efficient.

Moreover, the rise of sustainability and environmental consciousness has had a significant impact on the industrial landscape. Customers and stakeholders now demand greener and more sustainable practices from businesses. Industrialists need to develop strategies that not only minimize their environmental footprint but also enhance their brand image and reputation.

Additionally, the global marketplace has become increasingly competitive, with emerging economies challenging traditional industrial powerhouses. To succeed in this environment, industrialists must embrace a global perspective and be willing to explore new markets and partnerships. Collaboration and innovation are key to staying ahead of the curve and tapping into new opportunities.

However, it is not just external factors that are shaping the industrial landscape. The mindset of industrialists themselves plays a crucial role in navigating this changing terrain. It is imperative for industrialists to cultivate a growth mindset, embracing continuous learning and adaptation. They must be open to new ideas, willing to take risks, and embrace failure as a stepping stone to success.

Furthermore, industrialists need to foster a culture of agility within their organizations. The ability to respond quickly to market changes, customer demands, and technological advancements is paramount in today's fast-paced world. This requires a flexible and adaptive approach, where hierarchies are replaced by cross-functional teams, and decision-making is decentralized.

In conclusion, the current state of the industrial landscape is characterized by rapid technological advancements, increasing sustainability demands, global competition, and the need for a growth mindset. Industrialists must be proactive in embracing these changes, seeking opportunities for innovation and collaboration. By mastering the art of change, industrialists can position themselves at the forefront of the evolving industrial landscape and secure long-term success in a dynamic world.

Chapter 2: The Need for Adaptation and Change

Recognizing the Need for Adaptation

In today's rapidly changing world, the ability to adapt is crucial for success in any field, especially for those in the industrial sector. As an industrialist, it is essential to understand the importance of recognizing the need for adaptation and embracing change in order to stay competitive and thrive in a dynamic environment.

The mindset of an industrialist traditionally focuses on stability, efficiency, and long-term planning. However, with the ever-evolving technological advancements, market shifts, and changing customer preferences, it is no longer feasible to rely solely on established practices and strategies. The key to survival in this new landscape lies in recognizing the need for adaptation.

Adaptation is not about abandoning what has worked in the past, but rather about being open to new ideas, embracing innovation, and being willing to change course when necessary. It requires a shift in mindset from being resistant to change to being proactive and forward-thinking. By recognizing the need for adaptation, industrialists can position themselves to take advantage of emerging opportunities and mitigate risks associated with stagnation.

One of the first steps in recognizing the need for adaptation is staying informed about industry trends and developments. This can be achieved through continuous learning, attending conferences, networking with peers, and keeping abreast of technological advancements. By being aware of the latest changes in the industry, industrialists can anticipate potential challenges and be better prepared to adapt their strategies accordingly.

Additionally, it is crucial to foster a culture of adaptation within the organization. This involves encouraging employees to embrace change, empowering them to contribute their ideas, and creating an environment that rewards innovation. By fostering a mindset of adaptability, industrialists can tap into the collective intelligence of their workforce and stay ahead of the curve.

Recognizing the need for adaptation also requires a willingness to take calculated risks. This means being open to experimentation, learning from failures, and being agile in decision-making. Industrialists must be willing to challenge the status quo and explore new avenues to remain relevant in an ever-evolving market.

In conclusion, recognizing the need for adaptation is imperative for industrialists in today's dynamic world. By embracing change, staying informed, fostering a culture of adaptation, and taking calculated risks, industrialists can position themselves for success in an ever-changing landscape. The ability to adapt is not only a survival strategy, but also a key driver of growth and innovation. So, let us embrace the need for adaptation and become adaptive industrialists who can master change and thrive in the face of uncertainty.

Embracing Disruption in the Industrial Landscape

In today's rapidly evolving world, the industrial landscape is constantly being disrupted by technological advancements, changing consumer preferences, and global economic shifts. To thrive in this dynamic environment, industrialists must adopt a new mindset—one that embraces disruption rather than fearing it. This subchapter explores the concept of embracing disruption and provides valuable insights for industrialists who wish to master change and stay ahead of the curve.

Disruption, often associated with chaos and instability, can actually be a catalyst for innovation and growth. By embracing disruption, industrialists can unlock new opportunities, challenge traditional business models, and gain a competitive edge. However, this requires a shift in mindset—one that goes beyond adapting to change and instead seeks to proactively shape the future.

To begin embracing disruption, industrialists must cultivate a mindset of curiosity and continuous learning. They must be willing to explore new technologies, trends, and business models, and be open to experimenting and embracing failure as a stepping stone to success. By fostering a culture of innovation within their organizations, industrialists can encourage their teams to think outside the box and generate groundbreaking ideas.

Furthermore, embracing disruption requires industrialists to be proactive rather than reactive. Instead of waiting for external forces to disrupt their industries, they must anticipate and embrace change before it happens. This involves conducting thorough market research, monitoring trends, and staying informed about emerging technologies. By doing so, industrialists can position themselves as pioneers in their industries and be the ones driving change, rather than being left behind.

Another crucial aspect of embracing disruption is the ability to adapt quickly. Industrialists must be agile and flexible in their approach, willing to pivot and adjust their strategies as the market demands. This requires a certain level of resilience and a willingness to let go of outdated practices and embrace new ways of doing business.

In conclusion, embracing disruption in the industrial landscape is essential for industrialists to remain relevant and competitive in today's fast-paced world. By adopting a mindset of curiosity, continuous learning, and proactivity, industrialists can not only adapt to change but also drive it. By embracing disruption, they can seize new opportunities, challenge the status quo, and lead their industries into a future of growth and innovation.

The Dangers of Resisting Change

In today's rapidly evolving world, the ability to adapt and embrace change is crucial for individuals and businesses alike. However, many individuals, especially those with an industrialist mindset, often find themselves resistant to change. This resistance can be attributed to a variety of factors, such as fear of the unknown, comfort in the familiar, or a desire to maintain control. While it may seem tempting to cling to what is familiar, the dangers of resisting change can be detrimental to personal growth, professional success, and overall well-being.

One of the primary dangers of resisting change is stagnation. When we resist change, we are essentially refusing to grow and evolve. In an ever-changing world, this can quickly lead to falling behind competitors, missing out on new opportunities, and becoming irrelevant in our respective industries. The industrialist mindset, which often values stability and predictability, can exacerbate this danger. By resisting change, we are limiting our potential for innovation and preventing ourselves from adapting to the demands of a dynamic marketplace.

Additionally, resisting change can also lead to increased stress and frustration. Change is often accompanied by uncertainty, and our resistance to it can create a constant state of tension and anxiety. This can have detrimental effects on our mental and emotional well-being, as well as our ability to effectively navigate challenges and setbacks. Embracing change, on the other hand, allows us to develop resilience and the ability to thrive in uncertain circumstances.

Furthermore, resisting change can create a negative perception of us within our personal and professional networks. Those who resist change are often seen as stubborn, inflexible, and resistant to growth. This can hinder our ability to form meaningful relationships, collaborate effectively, and achieve long-term success. By embracing change, we demonstrate our willingness to adapt and learn, which can enhance our reputation and open doors to new opportunities.

To overcome the dangers of resisting change, it is important for individuals with an industrialist mindset to cultivate a growth mindset. This involves recognizing the value of change, embracing discomfort, and seeking out opportunities for personal and professional development. By adopting a growth mindset, industrialists can position themselves as adaptive leaders in their respective industries, staying ahead of the curve and driving innovation.

In conclusion, the dangers of resisting change are vast and far-reaching. It is essential for individuals with an industrialist mindset to recognize these dangers and actively work towards embracing change. By doing so, they can unlock their full potential, stay relevant in a rapidly changing world, and ultimately achieve long-term success.

Chapter 3: Developing an Adaptive Mindset

The Importance of a Growth Mindset

In today's rapidly evolving world, the ability to adapt and embrace change is crucial for success. This is particularly true for industrialists, who operate in an environment that is constantly evolving due to technological advancements, market shifts, and global competition. To navigate these challenges and thrive in the face of uncertainty, adopting a growth mindset is of utmost importance.

A growth mindset is a belief that abilities and intelligence can be developed through dedication, effort, and learning. It is the understanding that challenges are opportunities for growth, and setbacks are merely temporary obstacles on the path to success. This mindset empowers industrialists to continuously learn, innovate, and effectively respond to the ever-changing demands of their industry.

One of the key benefits of a growth mindset for industrialists is the ability to embrace change. Rather than being resistant or fearful of new technologies or market trends, individuals with a growth mindset view these changes as opportunities for personal and professional growth. They are open to learning new skills, adapting their strategies, and exploring innovative solutions. As a result, they are more likely to stay ahead of the curve and seize new opportunities that arise.

Furthermore, a growth mindset fosters resilience in the face of failure. Industrialists understand that setbacks are inevitable in any dynamic environment, and they view these failures as valuable learning experiences. Rather than becoming discouraged or giving up, they analyze their mistakes, make adjustments, and try again. This resilience enables them to overcome challenges, learn from their failures, and ultimately achieve their goals.

Additionally, individuals with a growth mindset are more likely to seek out feedback and collaborate with others. They understand the value of continuous improvement and recognize that the insights and perspectives of others can contribute to their own growth and development. By actively seeking feedback and engaging in collaborative efforts, industrialists can tap into a wealth of knowledge and expertise, enabling them to make better-informed decisions and achieve better outcomes.

In conclusion, cultivating a growth mindset is essential for industrialists in today's dynamic world. By embracing change, remaining resilient in the face of failure, and actively seeking feedback and collaboration, industrialists can continually evolve and adapt to the challenges and opportunities that come their way. Ultimately, a growth mindset is not only crucial for personal success but also for driving innovation, growth, and competitiveness in the industrial sector as a whole.

Overcoming Fear and Resistance to Change

Overcoming Fear and Resistance to Change: The Key to Mastering Change in a Dynamic World

Introduction:
Change is an inevitable part of life, and this holds true for every aspect, including the industrial sector. In today's fast-paced and ever-evolving world, adaptability is essential for survival and success. However, as industrialists, we often find ourselves grappling with fear and resistance when faced with the need to embrace change. In this subchapter, we will explore the underlying causes of this fear and resistance, and more importantly, how to overcome them. By mastering this crucial skill, we can unlock our potential as adaptive industrialists.

Understanding Fear and Resistance:
Fear and resistance to change are rooted in the human mindset. Our comfort zones, routines, and familiarity provide a sense of security, making change appear daunting. Additionally, the fear of the unknown, potential failure, and loss can further amplify our resistance. To become adaptive industrialists, we must acknowledge and understand these emotions, as they can hinder our progress and prevent us from seizing new opportunities.

Embracing a Growth Mindset:
To overcome fear and resistance, we must cultivate a growth mindset. This mindset thrives on continuous learning, improvement, and embracing challenges. By shifting our perspective from fear to curiosity, we can reframe change as an opportunity for growth.

Recognizing that failure is a stepping stone towards success allows us to approach change with resilience and perseverance.

Developing a Supportive Environment:
Creating a supportive environment is crucial in overcoming fear and resistance to change. By fostering open communication, encouraging collaboration, and celebrating small victories, we can build a culture of trust and empowerment. Industrialists must actively involve their teams in decision-making processes and provide them with the resources and training necessary for adapting to new technologies and practices. This collective approach helps dissipate fear and resistance, as it fosters a sense of ownership and collective responsibility.

Learning from Failure:
Change often comes with setbacks and failures. However, these should be viewed as valuable learning opportunities rather than deterrents. By embracing a growth mindset, we can extract lessons from our failures, adapt our strategies, and move forward stronger than before. Sharing these experiences with others creates a culture of learning and resilience, making change less intimidating and more manageable.

Conclusion:
As adaptive industrialists, we must recognize that fear and resistance to change are natural but surmountable hurdles. By cultivating a growth mindset, fostering a supportive environment, and embracing failure as a learning opportunity, we can overcome these barriers. The ability to adapt and embrace change is what separates successful industrialists from stagnant ones in a dynamic world. So, let us confront our fears, embrace change, and become masters of our own destiny.

Cultivating a Curious and Open Mind

In today's fast-paced and ever-changing world, cultivating a curious and open mind is crucial, especially for those with an industrialist mindset. The Adaptive Industrialist: Mastering Change in a Dynamic World emphasizes the importance of continuously learning and evolving to thrive in the face of constant change. This subchapter explores the significance of curiosity and open-mindedness as essential traits for industrialists navigating the complex challenges of our time.

Curiosity is the fuel that drives innovation and growth. It is the desire to explore, question, and understand the world around us. For industrialists, curiosity enables them to identify emerging trends, technologies, and opportunities that can shape the future of their industries. By maintaining a curious mindset, they can stay ahead of the curve, anticipate market shifts, and adapt their strategies to remain competitive.

Open-mindedness goes hand in hand with curiosity. It is the willingness to consider alternative perspectives, challenge assumptions, and embrace new ideas. In an era where disruption is the norm, industrialists must be open to unconventional solutions and approaches. By embracing diverse viewpoints, they can uncover innovative solutions to complex problems and foster a culture of collaboration within their organizations.

Cultivating a curious and open mind requires intentional effort. The subchapter explores various strategies to foster these traits, such as engaging in continuous learning, seeking out new experiences, and actively engaging with diverse communities. It encourages readers to step out of their comfort zones, attend industry conferences, participate in networking events, and initiate conversations with experts and thought leaders. By immersing themselves in different perspectives, industrialists can broaden their horizons and gain valuable insights that can inform their decision-making.

Furthermore, the subchapter emphasizes the importance of embracing failure as a learning opportunity. Industrialists must not fear taking risks but rather view failures as stepping stones to success. By adopting a growth mindset, they can learn from their mistakes, refine their approaches, and pivot when necessary.

In conclusion, cultivating a curious and open mind is essential for individuals with an industrialist mindset. The Adaptive Industrialist: Mastering Change in a Dynamic World encourages readers to embrace curiosity, open-mindedness, and continuous learning as key drivers of success. By adopting these traits, industrialists can navigate the ever-changing landscape, drive innovation, and stay ahead of the competition.

Chapter 4: Embracing Innovation in the Industrial World

The Role of Innovation in Adaptation

In the ever-evolving landscape of the modern business world, the need for adaptation has become more crucial than ever before. The ability to quickly respond to changing circumstances and embrace new opportunities has become the hallmark of successful industrialists. This subchapter explores the pivotal role that innovation plays in enabling businesses to adapt effectively in a dynamic world.

Innovation is not just about creating groundbreaking products or services; it is a mindset that embraces change and constantly seeks new ways to improve and evolve. Industrialists with an innovative mindset are not afraid to challenge the status quo and think outside the box. They understand that adaptation is not a one-time event but an ongoing process that requires continuous learning, experimentation, and improvement.

One of the key benefits of innovation in adaptation is the ability to identify and seize opportunities in rapidly changing markets. By staying attuned to emerging trends and technologies, industrialists can proactively adapt their business models to meet the evolving needs and demands of their customers. This proactive approach helps them stay ahead of the competition and maintain a competitive edge.

Furthermore, innovation fosters resilience in the face of uncertainty and disruption. Industrialists who embrace innovation are more likely to have diverse portfolios, allowing them to weather economic downturns and market fluctuations. By constantly exploring new avenues and diversifying their offerings, they can pivot quickly when unexpected challenges arise.

Innovation also enables industrialists to optimize their operations and processes. By integrating new technologies, streamlining workflows, and eliminating inefficiencies, businesses can become more agile and responsive. This not only improves their ability to adapt to external changes but also enhances their overall productivity and profitability.

Moreover, innovation promotes a culture of continuous improvement within an organization. When employees are encouraged to think creatively and contribute their ideas, they become more engaged and motivated. This collaborative environment fosters a collective intelligence that is better equipped to navigate complex challenges and adapt to changing circumstances.

In conclusion, innovation plays a pivotal role in enabling industrialists to adapt effectively in a dynamic world. By embracing an innovative mindset, businesses can identify and seize opportunities, foster resilience, optimize operations, and cultivate a culture of continuous improvement. In today's rapidly evolving landscape, businesses that fail to innovate and adapt run the risk of becoming obsolete. Therefore, it is imperative for industrialists to embrace innovation as a core value and leverage its power to master change and thrive in a dynamic world.

Embracing Technological Advancements

In today's rapidly evolving world, technological advancements have become an integral part of our daily lives. From smartphones to artificial intelligence, these innovations have revolutionized the way we work, communicate, and live. In the realm of industry, embracing these advancements is no longer an option but a necessity for survival and growth. The mind-set of an industrialist must adapt to this new reality, leveraging technology to stay ahead of the curve and remain competitive in a dynamic world.

One of the key reasons why industrialists must embrace technological advancements is the potential for increased efficiency and productivity. Automation, for example, has revolutionized manufacturing processes, allowing for faster and more accurate production. By incorporating robotics and other automated systems, industrialists can optimize their operations, reduce costs, and deliver products and services more efficiently. Embracing technology also opens up new avenues for innovation, enabling industrialists to explore novel solutions and disruptive business models that can propel them ahead of their competitors.

Moreover, technological advancements have the power to enhance safety and sustainability in the industrial sector. With the advent of smart sensors and Internet of Things (IoT) devices, industrialists can monitor and analyze data in real-time, identifying potential hazards, detecting equipment failures, and proactively addressing issues. This not only ensures a safer working environment but also reduces the risk of accidents and downtime. Additionally, embracing technology allows industrialists to adopt more sustainable practices, such as energy-efficient processes and waste reduction initiatives, contributing to a greener future.

However, embracing technological advancements requires a shift in mindset. Industrialists must be open to change, willing to learn and adapt to new technologies. They must foster a culture of continuous learning and innovation within their organizations, encouraging employees to embrace technological advancements rather than fearing them. This can be achieved through training programs, workshops, and collaboration with technology experts and start-ups. By nurturing a culture of curiosity and experimentation, industrialists can create an environment where embracing technological advancements becomes second nature.

In conclusion, the mind-set of an industrialist must evolve to embrace technological advancements in order to thrive in a dynamic world. These advancements offer opportunities for increased efficiency, innovation, safety, and sustainability. By being open to change and fostering a culture of continuous learning, industrialists can leverage technology as a catalyst for growth and success. Embracing technological advancements is no longer a choice but a necessity for industrialists who wish to remain competitive and relevant in today's ever-changing landscape.

Leveraging Data and Analytics

Leveraging Data and Analytics: Unlocking the Power of Information for Industrial Success

In the ever-evolving landscape of today's industrial world, the ability to adapt and thrive amidst constant change is crucial. This subchapter explores the importance of leveraging data and analytics as a means to master change and achieve success. Whether you are an established industrialist or someone aspiring to develop an industrial mindset, understanding the power of data and analytics can revolutionize the way you operate and navigate through the dynamic challenges of the modern business environment.

Data has become the lifeblood of industries, offering valuable insights and opportunities for growth. By harnessing the vast amounts of data generated within your organization, you can gain a competitive edge, make informed decisions, and drive innovation. However, the true value lies not only in collecting data but also in effectively analyzing and interpreting it.

Analytics plays a pivotal role in transforming raw data into actionable intelligence. By employing advanced analytics tools and techniques, industrialists can uncover hidden patterns, trends, and correlations within their data sets. This enables them to make data-driven decisions, optimize processes, and identify potential risks and opportunities. From supply chain optimization to predictive maintenance and customer behavior analysis, the possibilities are endless.

For every industrialist, embracing a data-driven culture is paramount. It requires a shift in mindset, where data becomes a strategic asset rather than an afterthought. By fostering a culture that values data and analytics, organizations can empower their employees to make evidence-based decisions, encourage innovation, and drive continuous improvement. Furthermore, data-driven decision-making creates a more transparent and accountable environment, fostering trust among stakeholders.

This subchapter also explores the challenges associated with leveraging data and analytics. From data privacy and security concerns to the need for skilled data professionals, industrialists must navigate through these hurdles to fully capitalize on the potential of data-driven practices. It also addresses the ethical considerations surrounding data usage, emphasizing the importance of responsible data management and privacy protection.

In conclusion, leveraging data and analytics is a crucial component of mastering change in the dynamic industrial world. By embracing a data-driven culture and effectively harnessing the power of information, industrialists can gain a competitive advantage, drive innovation, and achieve sustainable success. Whether you are an established industrialist seeking to enhance your operations or someone aspiring to develop an industrial mindset, understanding and harnessing the power of data and analytics will be indispensable in navigating the challenges and opportunities that lie ahead.

Chapter 5: Building Resilience in the Face of Change

Understanding the Impact of Change on Individuals and Organizations

Change is an inevitable part of life, and it affects every aspect of our existence. In the business world, change is not only constant but also essential for growth and survival. In "The Adaptive Industrialist: Mastering Change in a Dynamic World," we delve into the profound impact change has on both individuals and organizations, with a particular focus on the mindset of industrialists.

For individuals, change can be both exciting and challenging. It pushes us out of our comfort zones and forces us to adapt and evolve. The mindset of an industrialist, however, embraces change as an opportunity rather than a threat. It is this mindset that allows individuals to navigate through the uncertainties and complexities of change, leveraging it to their advantage. By understanding the impact of change on themselves, industrialists can proactively seek growth and innovation, continuously improving their skills and knowledge to stay ahead of the curve.

Organizations, on the other hand, face a unique set of challenges when it comes to change. The impact of change on an organization can be transformative, leading to either great success or catastrophic failure. Industrialists understand this and recognize the need for a strategic approach to change management. They foster a culture of adaptability and resilience, empowering their employees to embrace change and drive innovation.

In this subchapter, we explore the various dimensions of change and how it affects individuals and organizations. We delve into the psychological aspects of change, such as resistance and fear, and provide strategies for overcoming these barriers. We also examine the impact of change on organizational structures, processes, and systems, emphasizing the importance of agility and flexibility in a rapidly evolving business landscape.

Furthermore, we provide practical tools and techniques to help individuals and organizations navigate through change successfully. From identifying opportunities for growth to building a change-ready culture, we equip our readers with the knowledge and skills necessary to thrive in an ever-changing world.

"The Adaptive Industrialist: Mastering Change in a Dynamic World" is a comprehensive guide that addresses the unique challenges faced by industrialists in embracing and leveraging change. Whether you are an aspiring industrialist or an established one seeking to enhance your adaptability, this subchapter will provide you with valuable insights and practical strategies to become a master of change.

Developing Resilience Skills

Resilience is a crucial skill for individuals in any field, especially for those with the mindset of an industrialist. In the ever-changing and dynamic world we live in, the ability to adapt and bounce back from challenges and setbacks is essential for success. This subchapter explores the importance of developing resilience skills and provides practical strategies to cultivate this invaluable trait.

Resilience is the ability to withstand and recover from adversity, setbacks, and stress. It is not about avoiding or denying difficult situations, but rather about facing them head-on and finding ways to navigate through them. The mindset of an industrialist understands that challenges are not roadblocks, but rather opportunities for growth and improvement.

To develop resilience skills, it is important to first understand and accept that setbacks and failures are a natural part of life. Embracing a growth mindset allows us to view failures as learning experiences, enabling us to bounce back stronger. It is crucial to reframe challenges as opportunities for growth and development.

Another important aspect of developing resilience is building a strong support system. Surrounding yourself with like-minded individuals who share your mindset as an industrialist can provide invaluable support and encouragement when facing difficult times. Additionally, seeking mentorship from experienced individuals who have overcome similar challenges can provide guidance and inspiration.

Practicing self-care is also essential in developing resilience. Taking care of your physical and mental well-being enables you to better cope with stress and adversity. Engaging in activities that bring you joy, such as exercise, hobbies, or spending time with loved ones, rejuvenates your energy and helps build emotional resilience.

Furthermore, developing problem-solving and decision-making skills is crucial in building resilience. By adopting a solution-oriented approach, industrialists can navigate through challenges more effectively. Developing the ability to analyze situations objectively and make informed decisions helps in finding creative solutions to problems.

Ultimately, developing resilience skills is an ongoing process that requires patience, practice, and perseverance. By embracing challenges, building a support system, practicing self-care, and honing problem-solving skills, individuals with the mindset of an industrialist can develop resilience and thrive in the face of change.

In conclusion, resilience is a vital skill for individuals with the mindset of an industrialist. Developing resilience skills enables us to face challenges head-on, view setbacks as opportunities, and bounce back stronger. By embracing a growth mindset, building a support system, practicing self-care, and honing problem-solving skills, individuals can cultivate resilience and master change in a dynamic world.

Creating an Agile and Flexible Workforce

In today's rapidly evolving world, the success of any industrialist depends on their ability to adapt and respond to change. This requires not only a forward-thinking mindset but also a workforce that is agile and flexible. In this subchapter, we will explore the importance of creating an agile and flexible workforce and provide practical strategies for achieving this goal.

The mindset of an industrialist is crucial in cultivating an agile and flexible workforce. It starts with embracing change and seeing it as an opportunity rather than a threat. Industrialists must encourage their employees to adopt this mindset by fostering a culture of continuous learning and growth. This can be achieved through regular training programs, providing opportunities for skill development, and promoting a mindset of experimentation and innovation.

To create an agile and flexible workforce, industrialists need to empower their employees and give them a sense of ownership over their work. This can be achieved by encouraging autonomy and decision-making at all levels of the organization. By empowering employees to take ownership of their work, industrialists can foster a sense of accountability and motivation, leading to increased productivity and adaptability.

Another key aspect of creating an agile and flexible workforce is embracing technology and digital transformation. Industrialists must stay up-to-date with the latest technological advancements and leverage them to streamline processes and enhance productivity. This may involve investing in automation, artificial intelligence, and data analytics to gain insights and make informed decisions.

Furthermore, industrialists need to encourage collaboration and teamwork among their workforce. By fostering a culture of collaboration, employees can exchange ideas, share knowledge, and work together to solve complex problems. This promotes adaptability as employees learn from one another and collectively respond to changing market dynamics.

In addition, industrialists should be open to remote and flexible work arrangements. The COVID-19 pandemic has shown that remote work is not only possible but can also increase productivity and work-life balance. By embracing remote work, industrialists can attract and retain top talent from around the world, regardless of geographical constraints.

In conclusion, creating an agile and flexible workforce is essential for industrialists to thrive in a dynamic world. By fostering a forward-thinking mindset, empowering employees, embracing technology, promoting collaboration, and embracing remote work, industrialists can build a workforce that is adaptable, innovative, and capable of mastering change.

Chapter 6: Navigating Disruption in the Industrial Landscape

Understanding Disruptive Forces

In today's ever-changing world, it is essential for industrialists to understand and adapt to disruptive forces. These forces, which can come in the form of technological advancements, changing consumer preferences, or even geopolitical shifts, have the power to completely reshape industries and businesses. In this subchapter, we will delve into the concept of disruptive forces and explore how industrialists can develop the right mindset to navigate and thrive in a dynamic world.

Disruptive forces, by their very nature, can be unpredictable and highly impactful. They can emerge from unexpected sources and quickly transform the competitive landscape. The first step in understanding disruptive forces is to acknowledge that they are not temporary disruptions but rather permanent shifts that require long-term strategies. Industrialists must be willing to challenge conventional wisdom and embrace change as a constant.

To successfully navigate disruptive forces, industrialists need to cultivate a growth mindset. This mindset involves being open to new ideas, constantly learning, and actively seeking opportunities for innovation. It means being willing to take calculated risks and experiment with new business models. By adopting a growth mindset, industrialists can position themselves to spot and seize opportunities that arise from disruptive forces.

Another crucial aspect of understanding disruptive forces is staying informed and being proactive. Industrialists should closely monitor trends and developments in their industry and beyond. This includes keeping an eye on emerging technologies, changes in regulations, and shifts in consumer behavior. By staying ahead of the curve, industrialists can anticipate potential disruptions and take early action to mitigate their impact.

Collaboration is also key when it comes to understanding disruptive forces. Industrialists should actively seek out partnerships and collaborations with other stakeholders in their industry. By pooling resources and knowledge, industrialists can better respond to disruptive forces and share the risks associated with navigating uncertain terrain.

Lastly, industrialists must be adaptable and agile in their approach. They should be willing to pivot their strategies and make quick decisions when necessary. This requires a willingness to let go of outdated practices and embrace new ways of doing things. Industrialists who can adapt to change and quickly adjust their course will be better equipped to thrive in the face of disruptive forces.

In conclusion, understanding disruptive forces is crucial for industrialists in today's dynamic world. By cultivating a growth mindset, staying informed, collaborating with others, and being adaptable, industrialists can position themselves to not just survive but thrive amidst disruption. Embracing disruptive forces as opportunities for growth and innovation will enable industrialists to stay ahead of the curve and remain competitive in an ever-changing landscape.

Identifying Opportunities within Disruption

In today's rapidly evolving world, disruption has become the new normal. Industries are constantly being shaken up by new technologies, changing consumer behaviors, and emerging trends. For the mind set of industrialists, this can be both a challenge and an opportunity. In this subchapter, we will explore how to identify opportunities within disruption and thrive in a dynamic environment.

The first step in identifying opportunities within disruption is to embrace a mindset of flexibility and adaptability. As an industrialist, it is crucial to understand that change is inevitable and that resisting it will only hinder progress. Instead, view disruption as a chance to innovate and transform your business. This mindset shift will allow you to see beyond the immediate challenges and focus on the possibilities that lie within.

To identify opportunities, it is essential to stay informed and keep a pulse on the latest industry trends. By staying up to date with technological advancements, market shifts, and consumer preferences, you can spot potential gaps or areas ripe for innovation. Embrace a continuous learning mindset and invest in ongoing education to ensure you are equipped with the knowledge needed to identify and seize opportunities.

Networking and collaboration are also key in identifying opportunities within disruption. Engage with other industrialists, entrepreneurs, and experts in your field to exchange ideas and gain fresh perspectives. By fostering a network of like-minded individuals, you create a community that can support each other in navigating through disruptive times. Collaborative efforts can lead to the discovery of new business models, partnerships, or even completely novel approaches to solving industry challenges.

Furthermore, don't be afraid to experiment and take calculated risks. Disruption often requires thinking outside the box and challenging the status quo. Test new ideas, products, or services on a small scale before scaling up. By embracing a mindset of experimentation, failures become learning opportunities, and successes can lead to significant breakthroughs.

Lastly, always keep an eye on your customers and their evolving needs. Disruption often arises from shifts in consumer behavior or emerging trends. Regularly engage with your customers to understand their pain points and aspirations. By listening and adapting to their changing demands, you can position your business as a solution provider and stay ahead of the curve.

In conclusion, disruption can be a game-changer for industrialists. By adopting a mindset of flexibility and adaptability, staying informed, networking, experimenting, and focusing on customer needs, you can identify opportunities within disruption and thrive in a dynamic world. Embrace change, and let it fuel your innovation and growth as an adaptive industrialist.

Strategies for Thriving in a Disrupted Industry

In today's fast-paced and ever-changing world, industries are constantly being disrupted by new technologies, changing consumer demands, and global market shifts. As an industrialist, it is crucial to adopt a proactive mindset and equip yourself with strategies that will enable you to not only survive but thrive in this disrupted landscape. This subchapter explores some key strategies that can help you navigate and excel in a disrupted industry.

1. Embrace Change: The first and most important strategy is to embrace change wholeheartedly. Recognize that disruption is inevitable and that the only way to stay ahead is by adapting to new circumstances. Be open to new ideas, technologies, and ways of doing business. Cultivate a mindset of continuous learning and improvement.

2. Foster Innovation: Disrupted industries often require innovative solutions to stay relevant. Encourage a culture of innovation within your organization by empowering employees to think creatively and take risks. Invest in research and development to stay at the forefront of technological advancements. Collaborate with startups and other industry players to explore new business models and opportunities.

3. Customer-Centricity: In a disrupted industry, customer preferences can change rapidly. To thrive, it is essential to stay connected with your customers and understand their evolving needs. Invest in market research, data analytics, and customer feedback mechanisms to gain insights into their expectations. Tailor your products, services, and experiences to meet these changing demands.

4. Collaboration and Partnerships: Disruption often requires collaboration and partnerships to succeed. Look for opportunities to collaborate with other companies, both within and outside your industry. Joint ventures, strategic alliances, and partnerships can help you leverage complementary strengths and overcome challenges. Embrace an ecosystem mindset, where other players in your industry are seen as potential collaborators rather than competitors.

5. Agile Decision-Making: In a disrupted industry, time is of the essence. Develop an agile decision-making process that allows you to respond quickly to changing market dynamics. Empower your team to make decisions at various levels, decentralizing decision-making authority. Foster a culture of experimentation and learning from failures, enabling you to pivot and adapt as needed.

6. Talent and Reskilling: The skills required in a disrupted industry may differ from those traditionally valued. Invest in reskilling programs to ensure your workforce has the capabilities needed for the future. Encourage a growth mindset and provide opportunities for continuous learning and development. Attract and retain top talent by offering competitive compensation packages and a stimulating work environment.

By embracing change, fostering innovation, focusing on customers, collaborating with others, making agile decisions, and investing in talent, you will position yourself as an adaptive industrialist capable of thriving in a disrupted industry. Remember, disruptions also bring new opportunities. By staying ahead of the curve and proactively seeking ways to adapt, you can seize these opportunities and lead your industry into a more prosperous future.

Chapter 7: Leading Through Change and Uncertainty

The Role of Leadership in Times of Change

In today's fast-paced and ever-evolving world, change has become the new normal. The mindsets of industrialists must adapt to this dynamic environment if they wish to thrive and succeed. At the heart of this adaptation lies effective leadership. In this subchapter, we will explore the crucial role that leadership plays in navigating times of change and how it can shape the mindsets of industrialists.

Leadership is not just about managing people or resources; it is about guiding organizations through uncertainty and transformation. During times of change, leaders must provide a clear vision and direction that aligns with the evolving landscape. They must have the ability to anticipate and respond to emerging trends and challenges, while also inspiring and motivating their teams to embrace change.

One of the key responsibilities of leadership in times of change is to foster a mindset that embraces innovation and agility. Industrialists must be willing to challenge the status quo, experiment with new ideas, and adapt their strategies accordingly. Effective leaders create a culture that encourages creativity, risk-taking, and continuous learning. They empower their teams to think outside the box and explore new opportunities, even in the face of uncertainty.

Moreover, leaders must also be adept at managing resistance to change. Change can be unsettling and disruptive, often met with resistance from individuals who prefer the comfort of the familiar. Leaders must possess strong communication and interpersonal skills to address concerns, manage conflicts, and build consensus. They must create an environment where diverse perspectives are valued and encourage open dialogue to foster a sense of ownership and commitment to the change process.

In times of change, leadership is not limited to the top-level executives. Every individual within an organization has the potential to exhibit leadership qualities. By empowering employees at all levels and encouraging them to take ownership of their work, industrialists can create a culture of distributed leadership. This enables organizations to adapt more quickly and effectively to change, maximizing their chances of success.

In conclusion, leadership plays a pivotal role in shaping the mindsets of industrialists in times of change. It requires vision, adaptability, effective communication, and the ability to inspire and motivate others. By fostering a culture that embraces innovation, agility, and distributed leadership, industrialists can navigate the dynamic world with confidence and achieve sustainable growth.

Communicating Effectively During Transitions

In today's fast-paced and ever-evolving world, the ability to adapt and navigate through transitions is crucial for success. This is especially true for individuals with the mindset of an industrialist – those who are constantly seeking ways to innovate, improve, and thrive in their industries. However, mastering change requires more than just a willingness to adapt; it also requires effective communication skills to ensure a smooth transition.

Effective communication during transitions is essential because it helps to manage expectations, reduce resistance, and foster a sense of unity and purpose among all stakeholders. Whether you are implementing a new strategy, introducing a new technology, or undergoing a significant organizational change, here are some key principles to remember:

1. Transparency: Open and honest communication is the foundation of successful transitions. Be transparent about the reasons for the change, the expected outcomes, and the potential challenges. This builds trust and helps individuals understand the purpose behind the transition.

2. Active Listening: During times of change, it is crucial to listen to the concerns, opinions, and ideas of all stakeholders. Actively listen to their feedback, address their questions, and involve them in the decision-making process. This not only helps to identify potential roadblocks but also encourages ownership and engagement.

3. Clarity and Consistency: Clearly articulate the vision, goals, and expectations associated with the transition. Use simple and concise

language to avoid confusion and ensure everyone is on the same page. Additionally, be consistent in your messaging across all communication channels to prevent misunderstandings and reinforce key messages.

4. Empathy: Recognize that transitions can be challenging for individuals, and emotions may run high. Show empathy by acknowledging their concerns and providing support. Create a safe space for open dialogue and encourage individuals to express their thoughts and feelings.

5. Two-Way Communication: Communication should not be one-sided. Encourage an open dialogue where individuals feel comfortable sharing their ideas, concerns, and suggestions. Actively seek feedback and be responsive to it. This fosters a culture of collaboration and continuous improvement.

By following these principles, you can effectively communicate during transitions, ensuring that the mindset of an industrialist is embraced throughout the process. Remember, change is inevitable, but with effective communication, you can lead your organization, team, or yourself through transitions successfully. Embrace change, communicate effectively, and become an adaptive industrialist capable of mastering change in a dynamic world.

Building Trust and Inspiring Others

Trust is the foundation upon which successful relationships, businesses, and communities are built. In the ever-changing and dynamic world of industrialization, trust becomes even more crucial. As an industrialist, it is imperative to understand the significance of trust and its role in fostering innovation, collaboration, and growth.

Trust is earned through a combination of integrity, consistency, and transparency. By consistently delivering on promises, maintaining ethical standards, and being open and honest in all interactions, industrialists can establish a reputation for trustworthiness. This trust, once established, becomes a catalyst for inspiring others and creating a positive work environment.

Inspiration is the fuel that drives progress and innovation. As an industrialist, it is your responsibility to inspire your team, partners, and stakeholders to reach their full potential. By leading by example, setting ambitious goals, and encouraging creativity, you can ignite a sense of purpose and motivation within your organization.

One of the key ways to inspire others is through effective communication. Clear and concise communication helps to build understanding, align goals, and foster collaboration. By actively listening to your team members and creating an environment where everyone's voice is heard and valued, you can inspire a sense of belonging and ownership.

Another important aspect of building trust and inspiring others is recognizing and rewarding achievements. Celebrating successes, no matter how small, creates a positive and supportive culture. By acknowledging the efforts and contributions of individuals and teams, you not only boost their morale but also inspire others to strive for excellence.

Furthermore, as an industrialist, it is crucial to develop personal relationships with your team members and stakeholders. Building genuine connections based on trust and mutual respect fosters loyalty and commitment. By investing time and effort in understanding the needs and aspirations of others, you can tailor your leadership approach to inspire and empower them.

In conclusion, building trust and inspiring others are essential qualities for any industrialist. By embodying integrity, consistency, and transparency, you can establish a foundation of trust. Through effective communication, recognizing achievements, and developing personal relationships, you can inspire others to reach their full potential. As an industrialist, by mastering the art of building trust and inspiring others, you can navigate the dynamic world of industrialization with confidence and create a positive impact on both individuals and the industry as a whole.

Chapter 8: Harnessing Collaboration and Partnerships

The Power of Collaboration in Adaptation

In the fast-paced and ever-changing world we live in, the ability to adapt is crucial for success. This holds particularly true for industrialists, who face the challenges of an increasingly dynamic marketplace. To thrive in this environment, it is essential to embrace collaboration as a powerful tool for adaptation.

Collaboration, at its core, is the act of working together towards a common goal. It involves the pooling of knowledge, skills, and resources to achieve outcomes that would be difficult or impossible to attain alone. In the context of adaptation, collaboration enables industrialists to tap into a diverse range of perspectives and expertise, fostering innovation and agility.

One of the key benefits of collaboration in adaptation is the ability to leverage collective intelligence. No single individual has all the answers or possesses a monopoly on ideas. By collaborating with others, industrialists gain access to a wealth of knowledge and experience that can help them navigate the complexities of a rapidly changing landscape. This collective intelligence allows for more robust problem-solving and strategic decision-making.

Furthermore, collaboration promotes a culture of learning and continuous improvement. When individuals and organizations come together to adapt, they bring with them a variety of perspectives and approaches. Through collaboration, industrialists can share best practices, learn from each other's successes and failures, and collectively enhance their ability to adapt. This culture of learning not only benefits individual industrialists but also contributes to the overall development of the industry as a whole.

Collaboration also offers the opportunity to pool resources and share risk. In a world where uncertainty is the norm, collaboration allows industrialists to spread the burden of adaptation. By collaborating with others, they can share the costs and risks associated with experimentation and innovation, making adaptation more feasible and less daunting.

However, collaboration does not happen by chance. It requires a shift in mindset – a willingness to embrace openness, trust, and cooperation. Industrialists must recognize that collaboration is not a sign of weakness or dependency but rather a source of strength and resilience. They must be open to new ideas, be willing to listen and learn from others, and be proactive in seeking out collaboration opportunities.

In conclusion, the power of collaboration in adaptation cannot be underestimated. It enables industrialists to tap into collective intelligence, foster a culture of learning and continuous improvement, and share resources and risks. Embracing collaboration as a mindset and actively seeking out collaborative opportunities can help industrialists thrive in a dynamic world. By working together, we can master change and shape a future of sustainable success.

Establishing Strategic Partnerships

In the ever-evolving landscape of business, the ability to adapt and thrive in a dynamic world is crucial for success. This is particularly true for industrialists, who must navigate complex challenges and embrace change to stay ahead of the competition. One powerful tool in their arsenal is the establishment of strategic partnerships.

Strategic partnerships are collaborative relationships between two or more organizations that share a common goal or vision. These alliances can take many forms, from joint ventures and licensing agreements to supplier relationships and distribution partnerships. By joining forces with other entities, industrialists can leverage their collective strengths and resources to achieve mutual growth and innovation.

At its core, establishing a strategic partnership requires a shift in mindset. Industrialists must recognize that they cannot excel in isolation and that collaboration is essential for long-term success. By embracing this mindset, they open themselves up to a world of possibilities and opportunities.

One of the key advantages of strategic partnerships is the ability to access new markets and customer bases. By partnering with organizations that have a complementary customer profile, industrialists can expand their reach and tap into previously untapped segments. This not only leads to increased revenue but also fosters a deeper understanding of customer needs and preferences.

Furthermore, strategic partnerships enable industrialists to pool their resources and expertise. By combining forces, they can share the costs and risks associated with research and development, marketing campaigns, and infrastructure investments. This allows for faster and more efficient innovation, ultimately driving competitive advantage.

Another crucial aspect of strategic partnerships is the opportunity for knowledge transfer. Partnering with organizations from different industries or regions allows industrialists to gain fresh perspectives and insights. This cross-pollination of ideas can lead to breakthrough innovations and novel approaches to problem-solving.

However, establishing successful strategic partnerships requires careful planning and execution. Industrialists must identify partners that align with their values, goals, and capabilities. Building trust and open lines of communication is crucial for long-term collaboration. Additionally, a clear and mutually beneficial agreement should be established, outlining each party's roles, responsibilities, and expectations.

In conclusion, strategic partnerships are a powerful tool for industrialists looking to thrive in a dynamic world. By embracing collaboration, accessing new markets, pooling resources, and fostering knowledge transfer, industrialists can position themselves at the forefront of innovation and success. The key lies in adopting a mindset that recognizes the value of partnerships and actively seeking out opportunities to establish strategic alliances.

Leveraging Networks and Alliances

In today's rapidly changing world, the success of industrialists depends not only on their individual skills and knowledge but also on their ability to form and leverage networks and alliances. In this subchapter, we will explore the importance of building strong connections and collaborations, and how they can help industrialists thrive in a dynamic environment.

The mindset of an industrialist plays a crucial role in understanding the value of networks and alliances. Traditionally, industrialists have been known for their self-reliance and independent decision-making. However, the modern industrialist recognizes that no one can excel in isolation. By embracing a collaborative mindset, they understand the power of collective intelligence and the benefits of working together.

Building networks and alliances allows industrialists to tap into a vast pool of resources, knowledge, and expertise. By connecting with like-minded individuals and organizations, they can gain access to new ideas, technologies, and markets. Collaborations also enable industrialists to share risks and costs, making it easier to navigate uncertain and volatile business landscapes.

One way industrialists can leverage networks and alliances is through strategic partnerships. By forming alliances with complementary businesses, they can create synergies that drive innovation and growth. For example, a manufacturing company may partner with a technology firm to develop cutting-edge production processes. This collaboration not only enhances their competitive advantage but also opens up new market opportunities.

Another way to leverage networks is through mentorship and coaching relationships. By connecting with experienced industrialists who have successfully navigated similar challenges, aspiring industrialists can gain valuable insights and guidance. Mentors can help them avoid common pitfalls, accelerate their learning curve, and provide the necessary support to overcome obstacles.

Moreover, networks and alliances provide industrialists with a platform for continuous learning and development. Through conferences, industry associations, and online communities, they can stay updated on the latest trends, best practices, and regulatory changes. By actively participating in these networks, industrialists can exchange knowledge, share experiences, and contribute to the collective growth of the industry.

In conclusion, networks and alliances have become indispensable for the modern industrialist. By embracing a collaborative mindset and actively seeking out connections, industrialists can unlock a world of opportunities. Through strategic partnerships, mentorship, and participation in industry networks, they can leverage the collective intelligence and resources available to them. In this dynamic and ever-evolving business landscape, those who can effectively leverage networks and alliances will be the adaptive industrialists who truly master change and thrive.

Chapter 9: Overcoming Challenges in the Adaptive Journey

Common Challenges in Adapting to Change

Change is an inevitable part of life, and this holds true in the world of industrialists as well. In today's dynamic world, the ability to adapt to change is crucial for success. However, many industrialists find it challenging to navigate through these changes and embrace new ways of doing things. In this subchapter, we will explore the common challenges that industrialists face when adapting to change and provide insights on how to overcome them.

One of the primary challenges in adapting to change is the resistance to let go of old mindsets and practices. Industrialists often become comfortable with their established ways of doing things, which can hinder their ability to embrace new technologies, processes, or business models. It is essential to recognize that clinging to the past can limit growth and innovation. By cultivating a mindset of openness and curiosity, industrialists can overcome this challenge and be more receptive to change.

Another challenge lies in the fear of the unknown. Change often brings uncertainty, which can be intimidating. Industrialists may worry about the potential risks associated with new approaches or fear losing their competitive edge. To overcome this challenge, it is crucial to develop a growth mindset that views change as an opportunity for learning and improvement. Embracing a culture of experimentation and resilience can help industrialists navigate through uncertainties and adapt more effectively.

Lack of awareness and understanding of emerging trends and technologies is another common challenge. The industrial landscape is continuously evolving, and keeping up with the latest developments can be overwhelming. Industrialists need to invest time and resources in staying informed about industry trends, market shifts, and technological advancements. By staying ahead of the curve, industrialists can anticipate change and proactively adapt their strategies and operations.

Furthermore, a lack of communication and collaboration within an organization can hinder successful adaptation to change. Industrialists must foster a culture of open communication, where employees feel comfortable sharing ideas, concerns, and feedback. Collaboration across departments and with external partners can bring fresh perspectives and innovative solutions to the table, making change management more effective.

In conclusion, adapting to change is a significant challenge for industrialists, but one that is essential for survival and growth in a dynamic world. By addressing common challenges such as resistance to change, fear of the unknown, lack of awareness, and poor communication, industrialists can develop the mindset and strategies necessary to embrace change successfully. Remember, change is not a threat but an opportunity for innovation and progress.

Strategies for Overcoming Resistance and Obstacles

Introduction:
In the ever-changing landscape of the industrial world, it is crucial for every individual, especially those with the mindset of an industrialist, to equip themselves with effective strategies for overcoming resistance and obstacles. This subchapter aims to provide valuable insights and practical techniques to help navigate the challenges that arise when adapting to a dynamic world.

1. Embrace a Growth Mindset: To overcome resistance and obstacles, it is essential to cultivate a growth mindset. This mindset allows individuals to view setbacks as opportunities for growth and learning, rather than as failures. By embracing the belief that challenges can be overcome through effort and perseverance, industrialists can develop resilience and remain motivated in the face of adversity.

2. Foster a Culture of Innovation: Innovation is the key to staying ahead in a dynamic industrial landscape. By fostering a culture of innovation within their organizations, industrialists can encourage employees to think creatively, explore new ideas, and challenge the status quo. This mindset shift enables them to identify and overcome obstacles that may hinder progress.

3. Develop Effective Communication Skills: Clear and effective communication is crucial in overcoming resistance and obstacles. Industrialists should prioritize developing strong communication skills to effectively convey their vision, expectations,

and strategies to their teams. By fostering open and transparent communication channels, industrialists can build trust, resolve conflicts, and overcome resistance more efficiently.

4. Build Strategic Partnerships:
Collaboration is a powerful tool in overcoming obstacles. Industrialists should actively seek out strategic partnerships with like-minded individuals, organizations, and experts in their field. By leveraging collective knowledge and resources, they can overcome challenges more effectively and stay competitive in the market.

5. Embrace Technology:
Technological advancements have revolutionized the industrial landscape. Industrialists must embrace technology and continually adapt to the latest innovations to overcome resistance and obstacles. By staying updated on emerging technologies, industrialists can leverage automation, artificial intelligence, and data analytics to streamline processes, enhance productivity, and gain a competitive edge.

Conclusion:
Overcoming resistance and obstacles is a vital skill for industrialists operating in a dynamic world. By embracing a growth mindset, fostering a culture of innovation, developing effective communication skills, building strategic partnerships, and embracing technology, industrialists can navigate the challenges they encounter and emerge as adaptive leaders in their respective industries. By mastering these strategies, every individual with an industrialist mindset can thrive in an ever-changing business landscape.

Learning from Failure and Iterating

In the fast-paced and ever-changing world of business, failure is inevitable. However, it is not the failure itself that defines us, but rather how we respond to it. This subchapter, titled "Learning from Failure and Iterating," aims to guide the mindset of industrialists in embracing failure as a learning opportunity and utilizing the power of iteration to adapt and thrive in a dynamic world.

Failure is not something to be feared or avoided; instead, it should be seen as a stepping stone towards success. Every failure provides valuable lessons and insights that cannot be gained through success alone. By reframing failure as a necessary part of the journey, industrialists can transform setbacks into opportunities for growth and improvement.

One of the key principles of learning from failure is the concept of iteration. Rather than pursuing a linear path, industrialists should adopt an iterative approach that involves constantly testing, learning, and refining their strategies and solutions. By embracing this mindset, industrialists can adapt to changing circumstances and stay ahead of the curve.

Iteration requires a willingness to experiment, take risks, and challenge the status quo. It involves constantly questioning existing assumptions, seeking feedback, and making adjustments based on new information. Through a cycle of trial and error, industrialists can refine their ideas, products, and processes, ensuring continuous improvement and innovation.

To effectively learn from failure and iterate, industrialists must cultivate a culture of psychological safety within their organizations. This means creating an environment where employees feel empowered to take risks, share their ideas, and learn from their mistakes without fear of judgment or punishment. By fostering a culture that encourages experimentation and learning, industrialists can unlock the full potential of their teams and drive innovation.

Learning from failure and iterating is not a one-time process; it is a mindset that should be ingrained in every aspect of an industrialist's approach to business. By embracing failure, seeing it as an opportunity for growth, and constantly iterating, industrialists can navigate the complex and ever-changing landscape of the industrial world with confidence and resilience.

In conclusion, learning from failure and iterating is a crucial mindset for industrialists in today's dynamic world. By reframing failure as a learning opportunity, adopting an iterative approach, and fostering a culture of psychological safety, industrialists can harness the power of failure to drive continuous improvement and innovation. Embracing failure and iteration is not only the key to mastering change but also the path to long-term success in industrial endeavors.

Chapter 10: Sustaining Adaptation in a Dynamic World

Creating a Culture of Continuous Adaptation

In the rapidly evolving world of business and industry, the ability to adapt and embrace change is crucial for survival and success. The mindset of an industrialist plays a pivotal role in determining the fate of their organization in this dynamic landscape. To thrive in such an environment, it is imperative to foster a culture of continuous adaptation.

The concept of continuous adaptation goes beyond simply reacting to change; it involves proactively seeking out new opportunities and staying ahead of the curve. This subchapter in "The Adaptive Industrialist: Mastering Change in a Dynamic World" delves into the strategies and principles necessary to create such a culture.

First and foremost, it is essential to cultivate an open mindset among all members of the organization. Every individual, from the top-level executives to the frontline workers, should be encouraged to embrace change and view it as an opportunity for growth. By promoting a mindset of curiosity and continuous learning, employees will be more willing to experiment, take risks, and adapt to new situations.

Next, effective communication and collaboration are key to fostering a culture of continuous adaptation. Break down silos and encourage cross-functional teams to work together, sharing ideas and insights. This collaborative approach not only facilitates the flow of information but also encourages diverse perspectives and innovative thinking.

Furthermore, leaders must lead by example and actively support an adaptive culture. They should demonstrate a willingness to challenge the status quo, experiment with new ideas, and adapt their own strategies based on changing circumstances. By embodying the principles of continuous adaptation, leaders can inspire their teams to do the same.

Additionally, organizations should invest in creating a learning environment. This can be achieved through various means, such as providing ongoing training and development opportunities, supporting employees' pursuit of new skills, and fostering a culture of knowledge-sharing. By nurturing a thirst for knowledge and encouraging personal growth, organizations can develop a workforce that is adaptable and resilient.

In conclusion, creating a culture of continuous adaptation is vital for industrialists to thrive in today's rapidly changing world. By fostering an open mindset, promoting effective communication and collaboration, and investing in a learning environment, organizations can cultivate an adaptive culture that embraces change as an opportunity for growth. In "The Adaptive Industrialist: Mastering Change in a Dynamic World," readers will find practical strategies and insights to help them navigate the complexities of the modern business landscape and transform their organizations into agile and resilient entities.

The Role of Learning and Development

In today's rapidly changing world, learning and development play a crucial role in the success of individuals and organizations. In the book "The Adaptive Industrialist: Mastering Change in a Dynamic World," we explore the importance of continuous learning and development and how it can shape the mindsets of industrialists.

The mindset of an industrialist is characterized by a strong desire to innovate, adapt, and thrive in a dynamic environment. These individuals understand that in order to stay ahead, they must constantly update their knowledge and skills. Learning and development provide the tools and resources needed to keep up with the ever-evolving business landscape.

One key aspect of learning and development is the acquisition of new knowledge. By staying informed about the latest industry trends, technologies, and best practices, industrialists can make informed decisions and identify new opportunities. Continuous learning also allows them to anticipate future challenges and develop strategies to overcome them.

However, learning is not limited to acquiring new knowledge; it also involves developing new skills. Industrialists must be adaptable and possess a wide range of skills to navigate through various situations. Learning and development programs can help individuals enhance their problem-solving, communication, leadership, and critical thinking skills. These skills enable industrialists to lead effectively, collaborate with diverse teams, and drive innovation within their organizations.

Furthermore, learning and development fosters a growth mindset among industrialists. They understand that failure is a stepping stone to success and view challenges as opportunities for growth. By embracing a growth mindset, industrialists can overcome obstacles, take calculated risks, and continuously improve their performance.

Learning and development initiatives should be personalized and tailored to the specific needs of industrialists. Whether through workshops, seminars, online courses, or mentorship programs, individuals can choose learning opportunities that align with their goals and aspirations. Additionally, organizations should create a culture that encourages and supports continuous learning, providing resources and support for employees' professional development.

In conclusion, learning and development are fundamental to the mindset of an industrialist. By embracing a continuous learning approach, industrialists can stay ahead of the competition, navigate through uncertainty, and drive innovation in their industries. It is through ongoing learning and development that individuals can adapt to change, acquire new skills, and foster a growth mindset. In the dynamic world we live in, those who prioritize learning and development will be well-equipped to succeed and thrive.

Nurturing Long-Term Adaptation Strategies

In today's dynamic world, the ability to adapt is crucial for success in any industry. The mind set of an industrialist plays a significant role in determining their approach to change and their ability to thrive in a rapidly evolving business landscape. In this subchapter, we will explore the importance of nurturing long-term adaptation strategies and how industrialists can master change to stay ahead of the curve.

Adaptation is not a one-time event; it is a continuous process that requires a proactive mindset. Industrialists must cultivate an attitude that embraces change as an opportunity rather than a threat. This mindset shift is essential for developing long-term adaptation strategies that enable businesses to remain competitive and resilient in the face of evolving market dynamics.

One key aspect of nurturing long-term adaptation strategies is fostering a culture of innovation within the organization. Industrialists should encourage their teams to think outside the box, experiment with new ideas, and constantly seek ways to improve existing processes. By fostering a culture of innovation, industrialists can create an environment that is conducive to adaptability and agility.

Another crucial element of long-term adaptation strategies is the ability to anticipate future trends and disruptions. Industrialists must stay informed about industry developments, technological advancements, and changing consumer preferences. By closely monitoring these factors, industrialists can proactively identify potential challenges and seize emerging opportunities.

Furthermore, long-term adaptation strategies require industrialists to invest in continuous learning and development. They should encourage their teams to acquire new skills, stay updated on industry trends, and embrace a mindset of lifelong learning. By investing in the growth and development of their workforce, industrialists can ensure that their organizations are equipped with the necessary knowledge and capabilities to adapt to changing circumstances.

Ultimately, nurturing long-term adaptation strategies is about embracing change, fostering innovation, anticipating future trends, and investing in continuous learning. By adopting these strategies, industrialists can position themselves and their organizations for long-term success in an ever-evolving business landscape.

In conclusion, the mind set of an industrialist plays a pivotal role in their ability to adapt to change. By nurturing long-term adaptation strategies, industrialists can navigate the dynamic world with confidence and stay ahead of the curve. Embracing change as an opportunity, fostering a culture of innovation, anticipating future trends, and investing in continuous learning are all essential components of successful long-term adaptation strategies. By mastering change, industrialists can become adaptive industrialists and thrive in the face of uncertainty.

Chapter 11: The Future of the Adaptive Industrialist

Anticipating Future Trends and Disruptive Forces

In today's rapidly changing world, it has become crucial for industrialists to possess the ability to anticipate future trends and disruptive forces. As the world continues to evolve at an unprecedented pace, it is imperative for every industrialist to develop a forward-thinking mindset in order to stay ahead of the curve and thrive in this dynamic environment.

The concept of anticipating future trends involves closely monitoring and analyzing various factors that can potentially shape the industrial landscape. This includes keeping a keen eye on emerging technologies, market trends, consumer behavior, and global economic shifts. By staying informed and proactive, industrialists can identify potential opportunities and challenges before they arise, allowing them to adapt their strategies accordingly.

Furthermore, understanding and embracing disruptive forces is essential for industrialists to remain competitive. Disruptive forces can be defined as innovations or events that significantly alter the existing business models and industry dynamics. These forces can range from technological advancements and regulatory changes to shifts in societal values and environmental concerns. By recognizing and embracing disruptive forces, industrialists can position themselves to leverage these changes to their advantage, rather than being caught off guard and left behind.

The ability to anticipate future trends and disruptive forces requires a certain mindset. Industrialists must cultivate a sense of curiosity, adaptability, and a willingness to embrace change. They must be open to exploring new ideas, challenging the status quo, and continuously learning and evolving. By adopting an adaptive mindset, industrialists can effectively navigate the complexities of a rapidly changing world and seize the opportunities that arise.

In "The Adaptive Industrialist: Mastering Change in a Dynamic World," this subchapter aims to provide invaluable insights and practical strategies for industrialists to anticipate future trends and disruptive forces. It offers a comprehensive toolkit that encompasses market research methodologies, scenario planning techniques, and innovation frameworks to help industrialists stay one step ahead of the competition.

By embracing the content of this subchapter, every industrialist can develop the mindset and skills necessary to anticipate future trends and disruptive forces. By doing so, they can proactively shape their businesses to thrive in an ever-changing world, ensuring long-term success and sustainability. Whether you are an established industrialist or an aspiring entrepreneur, the knowledge shared in this subchapter will equip you with the tools needed to navigate the uncertainties of tomorrow and emerge as a true adaptive industrialist.

The Skills and Mindset of the Future Industrialist

In today's rapidly changing world, the industrial landscape is constantly evolving. To navigate this dynamic environment successfully, aspiring industrialists must possess a unique set of skills and a forward-thinking mindset. This subchapter explores the essential qualities that define the future industrialist, providing valuable insights for individuals aspiring to thrive in this challenging field.

One of the key skills required for a future industrialist is adaptability. As the industry continues to transform at an unprecedented pace, those who can quickly adjust their strategies, processes, and even business models will emerge as victors. The ability to embrace change, rather than resisting it, is crucial to stay ahead of the curve. A future industrialist must be open-minded and willing to explore new ideas and technologies to drive innovation within their industry.

Another critical skill for the future industrialist is technological proficiency. With advancements in automation, artificial intelligence, and data analytics, technological literacy has become a prerequisite for success. Industrialists must be able to leverage these tools effectively to optimize operations, improve productivity, and gain a competitive advantage. Moreover, they must continuously update their knowledge to keep pace with emerging technologies and trends.

In addition to technical skills, a future industrialist must possess strong leadership abilities. The industrial landscape demands individuals who can inspire and motivate teams, fostering a collaborative and innovative work culture. Effective communication, strategic thinking, and problem-solving skills are vital to navigate the complexities of the industry successfully. A future industrialist must also be adept at building and nurturing relationships with stakeholders, including employees, customers, suppliers, and investors.

A forward-thinking mindset is equally essential for a future industrialist. They must have a visionary outlook, constantly seeking opportunities to disrupt the status quo and push boundaries. This requires a willingness to take calculated risks, coupled with resilience to overcome setbacks. A future industrialist must possess a growth mindset, embracing failures as learning opportunities and continuously striving for personal and professional development.

In conclusion, the skills and mindset of the future industrialist are characterized by adaptability, technological proficiency, strong leadership abilities, and a forward-thinking outlook. These qualities are essential to thrive in the ever-evolving industrial landscape. By cultivating these skills and embracing the right mindset, individuals can position themselves as adaptive industrialists, ready to master change and succeed in a dynamic world.

Paving the Way for a Sustainable and Adaptive Future

In today's rapidly changing world, the need for industrialists to embrace sustainability and adaptability has never been greater. As we face the challenges of climate change, resource depletion, and technological advancements, it is essential that the mindsets of industrialists evolve to ensure a sustainable and adaptive future.

The concept of sustainability goes beyond environmental concerns; it also encompasses social and economic factors. Industrialists must recognize the interconnectedness of these three pillars and work towards creating a balance that supports long-term viability. By adopting sustainable practices, such as reducing waste, optimizing energy consumption, and investing in renewable resources, industrialists can minimize their impact on the planet while also improving their bottom line.

Adaptability is equally crucial in navigating the dynamic landscape of today's global markets. Technological advancements and shifting consumer preferences require industrialists to be agile and open to change. Embracing innovation and continuously improving their products and processes allows industrialists to stay ahead of the competition and meet the evolving needs of their customers. By cultivating a culture of learning and curiosity, industrialists can foster the flexibility and resilience necessary to thrive in a rapidly changing world.

To pave the way for a sustainable and adaptive future, industrialists must also engage in collaboration and knowledge-sharing. By working together with stakeholders, including governments, NGOs, and communities, industrialists can leverage collective expertise and resources to address complex challenges. Collaboration also fosters a sense of shared responsibility, promoting the development of innovative solutions that benefit society as a whole.

Education and awareness play a critical role in transforming the mindsets of industrialists. By understanding the implications of their actions and the potential consequences of inaction, industrialists can make more informed decisions that align with sustainable and adaptive principles. Investing in ongoing education and training programs that promote sustainability and adaptability can empower industrialists to lead by example and inspire others to follow suit.

In conclusion, paving the way for a sustainable and adaptive future requires a shift in the mindsets of industrialists. By embracing sustainability, adaptability, collaboration, and education, industrialists can contribute to a world that is not only environmentally conscious but also economically prosperous and socially inclusive. It is up to each and every one of us to recognize the urgency of the challenges we face and take action towards building a better future for generations to come.

Conclusion: Mastering Change in a Dynamic World

In this fast-paced and ever-evolving world, the ability to adapt and thrive amidst constant change is crucial. The industrialist mindset, characterized by a relentless pursuit of innovation and a passion for growth, is at the forefront of mastering change in this dynamic environment. Throughout this book, we have explored the key principles and strategies that can empower every individual to embrace change and become an adaptive industrialist.

One of the fundamental lessons we have learned is the necessity of having a growth mindset. The industrialist mindset is grounded in the belief that challenges and setbacks are opportunities for growth and development. By cultivating a mindset that embraces change, we can transform obstacles into stepping stones towards success. This mindset encourages continuous learning, experimentation, and a willingness to take calculated risks.

Another crucial aspect of mastering change is the ability to anticipate and respond to disruptions in the market. By staying attuned to emerging trends, technological advancements, and shifts in consumer behavior, the adaptive industrialist can position themselves ahead of the curve. This requires a commitment to ongoing research, collaboration, and a willingness to question conventional wisdom. It also means being open to new ideas and perspectives, and leveraging them to drive innovation.

Furthermore, effective communication and collaboration are essential for mastering change in a dynamic world. The industrialist recognizes the power of diverse perspectives and fosters an inclusive environment that encourages creativity and collaboration. By building strong networks and partnerships, we can tap into a wealth of knowledge and resources, enabling us to adapt quickly to changing circumstances.

Lastly, the adaptive industrialist understands that change is not a linear process, but rather a continuous cycle. It requires a willingness to embrace ambiguity, be flexible in our thinking, and constantly reassess our strategies. By being proactive in our approach to change, we can seize opportunities and turn challenges into advantages.

In conclusion, mastering change in a dynamic world is not just a skill reserved for a select few, but a mindset that anyone can adopt. By cultivating a growth mindset, staying ahead of disruptions, fostering collaboration, and embracing the cyclical nature of change, we can all become adaptive industrialists. The journey towards mastering change may not always be easy, but by embracing it wholeheartedly, we can navigate the tumultuous seas of change and emerge stronger and more resilient than ever before.